Girls Breaking The Mold

Dr. Angela Banner Joseph

Girls Breaking

The Mold

Illustration by Abira Das

Published by **Dr. Angela Marie Joseph**
Cover layout by **Stanley Joseph Leslie**

ISBN-10: 1-943945-05-5

ISBN-13: 978-1-943945-05-4

This book has been catalogued with the Library of Congress.

Printed in the United States of America

Also by Dr. Angela Banner Joseph

Two Nickels Holding Up a Dollar
I Am
YO SOY
Teaching Charlie the Value of a Dollar

Introduction

While reading this book of quotations, I hope you will begin to feel empowered as you learn about the meaning of leadership. The goal of the book is to prepare you to become a powerful and decisive leader in your home, school, and community while learning from women who came before you. I want to help you understand how leaders think about leadership and to help you build your leadership skills to benefit you throughout your life. I share the characteristics I believe inspire all girls to become exceptional leaders in their daily lives.

Young ladies, you must define your success by breaking the rules of the game. Your sisters worldwide have already shattered the so-called glass ceiling, so I challenge you to be more assertive, ambitious, passionate, and driven as you lead. The definition of leadership has many parts, which include figuring out what needs to be done, having the vision to solve the problem, and learning how to motivate people to achieve the goal.

I have provided this book of great leadership quotations from women who broke the mold. Like them, you may come from a different cultural background, have different experiences, and have more or different leadership skills than others have. You may become comfortable in your chosen leadership style, while others may not. Still, others may come from a unique cultural background, family situation, identity, or household income level. No matter what our family condition, we need to support and encourage each other to seek and attain key leadership positions.

We must continue to empower young women to lead because change occurs after you take action, and the action happens when you are inspired to lead. Now and in the future, you will transform yourself and others as you find the courage, skills, and passion for envisioning your community as a place where both genders are truly equal. Girls and women are slowly advancing into leadership positions in each community and country, but it is not enough. The changes have been slow and small. It is crucial that we continue to advance young girls and women into positions previously dominated by boys and men.

So, young ladies, what kind of leader are you? What are the things you already do, or you want to do, as a leader? How does your family's cultural background shape how you think about being a leader? Following are some personality traits of a girl or woman leader. Do you have any of these traits? The answer should be YES! I believe in you, so believe in yourself, and go for it.

Oprah Winfrey

"Surround yourself with only people who are going to lift you higher."

Helen Keller

"When one door of happiness closes, another opens; but often we look so long at the closed door that we do not see the one which has been opened for us."

Iyanla Vanzant

"The way to achieve your own success is to be willing to help somebody else get it first."

Alison Pincus

"Surround yourself with a trusted and loyal team. It makes all the difference."

First Lady of the United States
Michelle Obama

"As women, we must stand up for ourselves. We must stand up for each other. We must stand up for justice for all."

Katherine Miracle

"Do not wait on a leader... look in the mirror, its you!"

Bella Abzug

"Women have been trained to speak softly and carry a lipstick. Those days are over."

Muffet McGraw

"How you handle failure determines how successful you will be."

Constance Baker Motley

"Something which we think is impossible now is not impossible in another decade."

Anne Sweeney

"Define success on your own terms, achieve it by your own rules, and build a life you're proud to live."

Rules of Success

Indira Gandhi

"There are two kinds of people, those who do the work and those who take the credit. Try to be in the first group; there is less competition there."

Eleanor Rosalynn Carter

"You have to have confidence in your ability, and then be tough enough to follow through."

Mary Kay Ash

"Don't limit yourself. Many people limit themselves to what they think they can do. You can go as far as your mind lets you. What you believe, remember you can achieve."

Diane Sawyer

"Whatever you want in life, other people are going to want it too. Believe in yourself enough to accept the idea that you have an equal right to it."

Melinda Gates

"A woman with a voice is by definition a strong woman. But the search to find that voice can be remarkably difficult."

Ayan Rand

"The question isn't who's going to let me; it's who is going to stop me."

Coco Chanel

"In order to be irreplaceable one must always be different."

Martina Navratilova

"I think the key is for women not to set any limits."

Mother Jones

"My address is like my shoes. It travels with me. I abide where there is a fight against wrong."

Audre Lorde

"When we speak we are afraid our words will not be heard or welcomed. But when we are silent, we are still afraid. So, it is better to speak."

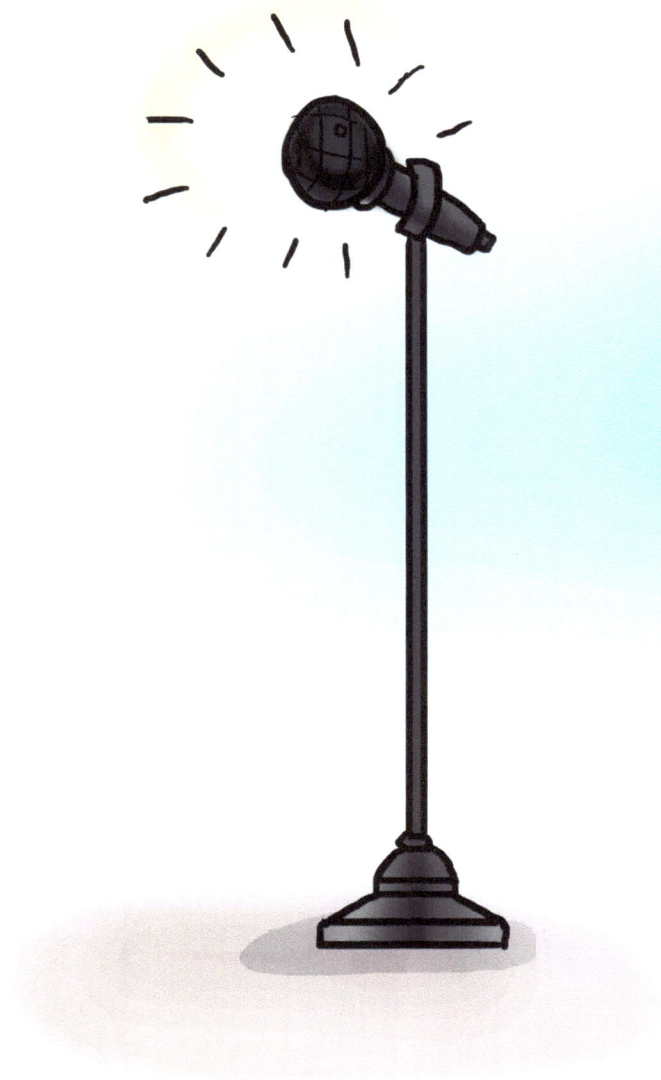

Dr. Angela Banner Joseph was born in Belize, Central America and has been employed at the City University of New York School of Law since 1991 as Director of Financial Aid. She earned her doctorate from the School of Educational Leadership for Change at the Fielding Graduate University, Santa Barbara, California. Dr. Joseph received a Master of Arts degree in Urban Affairs from Queens College of the City University of New York and a Bachelor's Degree in Sociology from the State University of New York at Stony Brook. She lives in New York City.

Thank you for purchasing this book. I am grateful.
You can reach me at Dr.AngelaJoseph@gmail.com or
visit Drangelabannerjoseph.com

www.ingramcontent.com/pod-product-compliance
Lightning Source LLC
Chambersburg PA
CBHW060814090426
42737CB00002B/59